CW00862764

Leadership and . . .

Adrian L. Hawkes

New Wine Press

New Wine Press
PO Box 17
Chichester
West Sussex PO20 6YB

First published in 1987 by N.L.M. Publications, Finsbury Park,
London N4.

ISBN: 0947852 88 3

By the same author:
 Attracting Training Releasing Youth, New Wine Press, 1992

Typeset by CRB Associates, Reepham, Norfolk
Printed in England by Clays Ltd, St Ives plc.

Dedication

Thanks to my family for their help and encouragement: Pauline, Anna, Carla and Gareth. I promised to mention their names.

Thanks to:
- my mother and father for their guidance in early years,
- Lesley, my secretary,
- Sally, for the illustrations,
- my mother-in-law for the use of a quiet place, namely her flat, to write in, and
- especially to Brian Brookes who said 'Why don't you write a book about Leadership?'

Here it is...

Contents

Foreword

Most books give a better impression of the writer and his work than the author readily deserves. It is much easier to put concept ideas and projects on paper than to work them out in relationships.

The reason I have been so happy to write the foreword to this book is simple: Adrian Hawkes has, in terms of friendship, quality of leadership, projects, educational forums and multi-racial churches, done more in reality than this publication might express.

Adrian Hawkes is a man of integrity, faith and wisdom with a devotion to Jesus and people. The home and family reflect this any day or afternoon you care to drop in. Whilst this is another contribution to leadership discussion it is a vital one and for this reason there is more to the man, his ministry and achievement than his writing conveys; surely an improvement on books that convey more than reality itself. Read, learn and digest and then maybe take a trip to North London and see. You will not be disappointed. God's love is everywhere in their work.

Gerald Coates

A Potted History

Thirty-five years ago Adrian Hawkes decided that the church needed stretching, bouncing, and shaping up, for the kingdom is waiting to express and fly free, so he rolled up his sleeves and grabbed the vision that **God** had given him: to make people ready to stand and fight for kingdom living.

It all started for him at the tender age of nineteen years, when as a young whipper-snapper he was asked to help with the youth in Sparkbrook, Brummiland. At first he started to push it away and reject the thought and title of shoulder-scraping responsibility. God thought otherwise.

Through pushing, screaming, kicking, and shoving, Adrian Leslie Hawkes finally jumped into leadership and, as it turned out, he became pretty good at it! He was becoming, in some people's perspective, the modern challenger of religious society.

He started to be at the forefront of youth culture in his area, with some of the 'establishment' walking out in disgust at the advent of the use of drums. Apparently it gave great offence to the Hammond organ and its piano companion. Underground culture was an opening for his work with the 'Ribbonette band' (a band he started in the sixties), music coffee bars, working men's clubs in the North Midlands, and many other alternative happenings. His leadership team began to grow. A 400-strong meeting in the centre of Birmingham at St Martins in the Bullring (financed by Anglicans), was run by a versatile team made up of all sorts of churches (who had many clashing perspectives). It was attended by rockers, next to the vegetable market, and if they didn't like the show they threw stinky, rotten vegetables at the stage.

That little bit of spice in his life has helped him through the rough and the smooth, and even now he manages to keep the youthful enthusiasm which has accompanied him throughout his calling within leadership and King-serving.

After working in the Midlands, Surrey, and North-East, he came over to the kebab shop land of North London in 1974. There he challenged the mindsets of the charismatic people by starting a culturally relevant, constantly changing, initiative bursting, new form of gathering called RAINBOW CHURCHES.

There he has started such direction-assisted works as Christian education (a schooling project with the principles of producing passionate, individual leaders), and a building programme that houses around sixty people and which also involves employing a couple of hundred people (enhancing their opportunities in the recession job market).

Through all these busy spells of down and up projects and encouragement, Adrian Leslie Hawkes and Pauline Anne Hawkes raised two daughters (who are both happily married and in alternative leadership) and one son who does alternative leadership in everything that's anything. Also, with the resource of social services, the Hawkes family extended their home further to facilitate fostering with teenagers, toddlers, and teeny boppers. As Mr Hawkes says, 'Biblical families were always extended families.'

Leadership – Serving – he mixed them like bread and wine. May more passion urgers follow from this man's experience.

Zippy Urger

Preface

This is an attempt to put the thoughts about leadership that I find basic and practical into book form. I suppose I could have gone into great detail in each chapter but then you might not have read it. In some ways, what I have tried to do here is to give you the bones of what I believe. It is a very important subject that we need to get hold of. Everywhere there is a strong need for leadership. God uses men and women, very rarely committees and bureaucracy. The times demand that we move forward with strong leadership. I hope my small contribution will help towards that end, towards the extension of the Kingdom and the glory of His name. And so let's lead.

Adrian L. Hawkes
New Living Ministries
North London

Chapter 1

Leadership and What It Is
A definition

I'm writing these things down because I know that they are important. It is important for many of us to understand them. All over the world at the moment we are crying out for leaders; in politics, business, education, the media and particularly in church life. That's not to say that there aren't any leaders, just not enough of them.

First to help us find, understand and promote leadership, maybe in ourselves, and perhaps to recognise it in others, we need to know what it is. Certainly we need to know what it is not, whatever is credited as being leadership elsewhere. In a church context we must get it right.

A leader is not a leader simply because he has been appointed to a position or because he has obtained a title by whatever means. Reverend by name does not make you reverend by nature, no more than parking yourself in a garage makes you a car. Leaders are not found by election, though they may be elected afterwards. They do not become **real** leaders simply because they think they should lead.

Some people tragically claim to be leaders, but one only has to see that people don't listen to them, follow them, obey them or in any way look up to them. They are a problem mainly to themselves for they are leaders without anyone to lead. If you look around you will discover that these people really do exist.

Just giving yourself a title or calling yourself a leader doesn't actually do anything.

So what does a leader do?

In the first instance leaders are men and women of God's appointment. There are very obvious things that will denote a leader. He will be the sort of person that others follow. Ever seen an appointed leader that people don't follow? It's not funny but embarrassing.

A pastor was heard to say one day to a fellow traveller, 'To get on in my church I watch carefully to see which way the people are going and then I follow them hard.' Whatever he was, he was not a leader.

You only have to look at the average group of youngsters on the street corner and immediately, with very little perception, you can pick out a leader. He or she is the person the rest of the crowd is following, looking up to, being obedient to.

You will sometimes see another funny side; self-imposed leaders with no-one following. They have great aspirations; they long to get there; they know they've got it; they are sure it's their responsibility.

Put simply: a leader is one who leads and who others will follow!

'To get on in my church, I watch carefully to see which way the people are going and then I follow them hard.'

Chapter 2

Leadership and Decisions
Decision makers

No-one who wants to be a leader can do so unless they have learned to make **decisions**! There are times to wait on God, times to take advice, times to become aware of the various opinions but there must be a time to act; to decide; to go.

People who never know, are never sure, who say things like, 'well I don't know,' 'well, I don't mind if it's this or that' are not leaders in the true sense of the word.

Decision-making is always a risk business. There are often no easy options. Many times there is no concrete guarantee of short-term success. All that you can be sure of is that God is with you and He's not leaving and there is an ultimate success to *'those who are called according to His purposes,'* but it might mean the next decision will bring the sky tumbling down.

Alan Vincent, a friend of mine, said 'the god of the United Kingdom is the god of security.' We, in England, are so worried about mortgage repayments, pension funds, retirement benefits, insurance arrangements, risk elimination that we have lost the ability, the pleasure, the joy of just living. Another friend of mine, George Canty, said 'one thing is sure, God has put us here to live.' So we should at least do that. Jesus said (He's another friend of mine), *'I am come that you might have life and that you might have it more abundantly,'* in other words the good life. We have changed all that to, 'I don't want life but a good pension, and to be insurable.' It's taken the living out of life. Don't even mention the word 'risk' or 'danger'.

Have you ever noticed how many children take risks for fun, climb the tree, stand on the ice? I'm not saying that they don't need adult protection but they are risky livers. Well, of course, there are accidents but they are alive to life. No risk, no leader; no decision, no leader. It is the very stuff of leadership.

Oh, and don't forget you can be wrong. The fear of a mistake, the fear of being wrong prevents many of us from being where God wants us to be. God won't knock us on the head. He has promised to give us wisdom, to forgive us when we confess our sins. He is the Heavenly Father.

Just as we would pick up a child who is learning to walk when they make a mistake and trip, so will the Heavenly Father. He is the picker-upper supreme.

Wrong decisions have to be faced. Sometimes they have to be turned round on. Most times it isn't only God who has to be confessed to. It is the people we lead.

'Please, please, make a decision, even if it's a wrong one.'

Leaders can be wrong and people, real people know that. People know it, even if leaders don't always and usually, if you're leading in a God-ordained way and have taught people well, they won't kill you for being wrong. Good people will forgive the genuine wrong decision, even if, as sometimes does happen, you have to live with that real wrong decision, and people have to live with it too ... for a very long time.

I had to laugh one day in a Church Board meeting, after something had been discussed for the umpteenth time, when one of our Board Members (a good man named Cyril Kabenla) said, 'Please, please make a decision, even if it's a wrong one.' If you step out of the boat you might sink, you might drown, you might get wet, but you could be walking on water. Leaders make decisions!

Chapter 3

Leadership and Attitude
Servant thinking

'And Jesus took a towel and girded himself around the waist. He filled a basin with water and washed the disciples feet.'

Not only did he do it, Jesus said,

'When the heathen rule or lead they lord it over the people but that should not be so with you. Whoever would lead must be the servant of all.'

Servant thinking is the secret of good leadership. It will take away that 'I must always be on the platform approach,' 'I must have my say' approach, 'I must prove I'm in charge' approach.

It will enable us to relax, to be in honour preferring one another, to encourage new and up-coming leadership, to give place on our platforms for others to exercise their God-given ministry and gifts, to rejoice when others do what we do and do it better. That's hard isn't it? To rejoice when others are in the midst of success and we don't seem to have grasped it yet. We shall feel less and less the need to be assertive ourselves, probably covering that inferiority complex, that fear of 'if so and so comes and preaches and they are better than me, what will happen to me? No-one will want me then.'

A servant is there to serve and all the other things I've just mentioned don't come into it. We just serve with or without praise, with or without thanks, with or without just reward, with or without success. Servants serve; that's what they do. To lead in the Kingdom of God we are commanded to have such a heart.

I've always remembered working in some special meetings with George Canty. He had been greatly used of God in healing the sick and in words of knowledge. I said to him 'Why doesn't God speak to me that way?' In his usual curt way (he was always to the point) he said, 'He would if you listened.' I said, 'Well, often I do think God has spoken to me, but I don't tell others.' 'Why not?' came the curt response. 'Well, I might be wrong or mislead.' Again a blunt question, 'So what?' 'Well,' said I, 'what would people think?' 'About what?' he asked. 'Well, about me,' said I. 'And who are you anyway?' he said. End of conversation.

I got the picture; I got the point. Oftentimes we are far more worried about what people think about us than ever we are about what God thinks about us. We don't have a servant heart do we? That is not to say that we should not be concerned as to what people think about us but we need to be most concerned about what God thinks.

There are things that we need to understand about a servant. A servant has real power. A good servant knows how things are done. A good servant can be trusted by the master with great responsibility. A good servant ends up being in charge.

Consider the story of Joseph in Potiphar's house, or better still in Pharaoh's court. As a good servant he had power over all that there was. A good servant isn't someone who is to be kicked about and treated like a doormat. A good servant is a highly valued prize, one who is trustworthy, one whom you would put in charge, someone who will call the shots, give the orders, be wise with advice, will have understanding of the situation.

In the Roman times of Paul a servant would often be put in charge of a son and would have more power than the son, until the son reached the age of maturity at which stage the father would adopt the son into the family giving him the full rights of a son. It was apparently possible if you had a particularly worthless son, a ne'er-do-well, one who had obviously given the servant in charge the run-around all the time, for the father to choose to adopt the servant and give him the rights of a son, and leave the son out in the cold.

Because of the servant's power, if the servant doesn't do the job, the job doesn't get done. So if your servant car won't start you'll be late for work. If the servant washing machine doesn't work you won't get clean clothes. By not doing what the servant knows to do, great disservice is caused to the master's plan for the servant's actions.

If you want to be leaders in the Kingdom you need to understand and apply this very basic principle of leadership. Want to lead? Learn to serve. Get servant thinking inside you.

Having said all that, remember also that Jesus then said, *'I no longer call you servants but friends,'* for a servant does not always know what the master is doing, or is planning to do, but these things are shared with a friend. I want to be a good servant, a good leader, but most of all I want to be his friend.

Chapter 4

Leadership and its Material
People: the stuff we work with

A little boy was being driven by his mother one day along the motorway. In front of them was a large lorry filled with lots of rubbish. It was obviously not going far, as the driver persuaded his mate that instead of going to all the trouble of tying down the tarpaulin sheet to cover the goods in the lorry, he should spread-eagle himself on top of the load to keep the tarpaulin sheet down.

The little boy with his mother driving behind the lorry looked up at the still, almost lifeless form of the driver's mate, when suddenly a gust of wind lifted one corner of the tarpaulin, causing the mate to react quickly to bring the large sail under control by throwing his arm over the offending, flapping corner. The little boy turned to his mum and said in a horrified voice, 'Look

Mummy, somebody has thrown away a perfectly good man.'

We must be very careful not to throw away perfectly good people. Jesus will not quench a smoking flax nor break a bruised reed.

Many times we are tempted to throw people away because they're not clever enough, or too clever by half, the wrong colour, the wrong culture, funny, silly, awkward, weird or whatever.

The stuff leaders work with is people and we need to get them motivated, activated, committed and following our leadership. We will not do that by being intolerant and throwing them on the scrap heap in our thoughts.

Of course some people will not learn and you will not be able to help them. Someone else might, but you must be careful not to throw them away! Bible history generally is full of success stories from people whom others had thrown away. You will, if you want to, discover that there are people whom others have thrown away that, if taken and carefully led and polished, will turn into diamonds whose bright light will dazzle you. These, you will find from careful handling, will not only become useful to the Kingdom, but even powerful leaders in their own right.

Leaders have to lead people. We will do all in our power therefore to learn to manage them;

direct them, not to deride them; generally to help them in whatever way possible to catch our vision. You'd better have one! You need other people to own your goals. You'd better be going somewhere if you want them to follow. Principally you need to make them your offering of worship to God, introducing them to the One who knows the value of every person very, very much. He's never willing to discard them, only if they throw themselves away. Jesus died for people and don't you forget it!

Many times we are tempted to throw people away.

Chapter 5

Leadership and Difficult People
Awkward ones

Have you ever had the situation where someone is difficult? You are struggling so hard to help and all you meet with is rebuff and hurt. A good leader will often ask himself, 'What am I doing wrong?'

Often times the leader isn't doing or saying anything wrong but in fact the response he's getting is wrong!

We need to know that the response may be wrong for all sorts of reasons, some which may have nothing to do with the leader. The thought that says, 'Perhaps it's me that is wrong' doesn't hurt for us to ask. It doesn't hurt us to say, 'Am I doing something wrong? Is there something I don't know, something I did not hear, something of my approach that is causing great difficulty?'

It doesn't hurt to ask those questions but

here are some questions that will restore your confidence in God and yourself and encourage you if you ask them:

1. Is the difficulty that I am having with this person something peculiar to me or are other people having the same problems? If others are having the same difficulty, don't blame yourself. The need, responsibility or difficulty lies somewhere else and not with you; you will just have to find it.

2. Is the difficulty or problem that we are seeing, the real problem or is it something else – at home, school, work or in their physical condition? It might need a word of knowledge from the Holy Spirit to come to a conclusion on that one, as often it won't be obvious.

3. Having asked these questions then you will have ascertained the problem. Then prescribe a cure! Sometimes it may be only the first step to a complete restoration of the person. If it took them twenty-five years to get in a mess you won't sort them out completely in three hours, not that I would recommend three-hour sessions of counselling anyway.

Sometimes even though people are saved, delivered, baptised in the Holy Spirit, have the right attitude to money and are going on with God, nevertheless a leader will sense that there is still a great distance to go and a wise leader will not expect a person to make a huge leap across the years like a streak of lightning. Rather the prescribed cure will be a teaspoonful of a large lake.

I suggest such things as 'I want you to read these verses of Scripture over and over again for the next seven days and then come and see me and I'll tell you the next step.' People must do the basics in the Christian life if they want to progress. So many want short cuts. There aren't any! It doesn't hurt to start with things like 'read the Bible regularly, talk to the Father at least once or twice a day, get at least twice-weekly strong Christian fellowship and other such curative medicine.'

Some people will run away when you've prescribed a cure. That's sad, but Jesus did not run after the rich young ruler who went away sorrowful, nor did He adjust the cure for something else. He just let him go, and sometimes leaders have to do just that. However, let's say yours doesn't run away.

4. What next will ascertain that the patient is taking the medicine? You have to find ways of checking that, because if it's your God-given medicine that has been given and then put on the shelf and not taken by the patient, they won't get better, and if they don't get

better they will get worse but that isn't the end of the world!

Usually when they get worse they come back to the person who has been loving and firm not the one who tried to be sickly nice and give them the easy option or the advice that they were looking for. Jesus was often not nice but He was always lovingly truthful.

Finally be careful your patient is not visiting a multitude of counsellors or leaders looking for advice that just suits them. Even if they get it, it won't help. Very often leaders need to decide 'Is this person my sheep, my responsibility?' before stretching themselves to meet the need. Otherwise we will spread ourselves so thinly we will achieve very little. A little story illustrates the point:

> I was working on a youth camp in the North of England, Fraisethorpe, by Bridlington. The camp had certain rules, and being one of the new leaders to join the camp staff I was not aware of one of those particular rules. One day a group of young people came to me and asked my permission to do something. Not being aware of the rules, their suggestion didn't sound too bad to me. Checking that there was an older person present I gave them permission to go ahead with their proposed plan.

A little later to my horror I discovered I was the last member of staff to be asked in a leadership team of about thirty people. Everyone else had said 'no,' I had said 'yes.' As you might imagine my other colleagues caused the sky to fall on my head. We need to ascertain very often just who else our patient is going to and try and keep good lines of communication open with other leaders.

Well, good counselling and I hope the sky doesn't fall in on you like it did on me.

Chapter 6

Leadership and a Small Group
Small groups

Jesus had many, many disciples and out of them he chose twelve. Out of those there were three and John the Beloved was really close in. Out of the nations God chose a man named Abraham. So you might ask if God has favourites. Well, sort of yes, but His plan is bigger than that. He plans to bless all who will be blessed. So God says to Abraham, 'I will bless (make you happy) so that in you all the nations of the earth will be blessed (made happy).'

So Jesus takes one, three, twelve and turns the world upside down or rather the right way up. You can only lead thousands as you lead a small group. Your vision must be infected on the larger from the smaller. Deal with one to cause a knock-on effect to another and another and another and another!

Even a small group will be made up of different personalities. There will probably be the shy ones. You could almost miss them or forget them, but if you'll spend time with them, encourage by word as well as action, give a small responsibility here and a big thank you there, then you will be so thrilled to see them open up and develop – and you will have played a part.

One of my greatest thrills in the first church I ever ministered in was to see a young lady who told me that the only thing she ever did was to wash up. That was her ministry to the body of Christ. I began to operate my own policy of a little bit more responsibility and encouragement here and there. It's thrilling to see her today going on with God in leadership along with her husband, doing things that she always said were impossible for her to achieve. Don't throw people away; use them and use the creative power of the Holy Spirit to create wonderful new people in God.

Sadly many preachers are happy with what I call 'worm preaching', that is telling people how bad they are. The funny thing is most people are already aware of their failures. Jesus, on the other hand, stretches out a hand and desires to lift up and make people into prophets, priests and kings. Leaders need to have the same perspective. Be a 'lifter-upper' of people and not a 'pusher-downer'.

Also your small group will possibly have the one who always wants to monopolise, take over every show, put the rest right, be noisy and loud. These sort don't need crushing. They do need channelling. Often they have got a good work output. You just need to get them in the right flow.

'I began to operate my own policy of a little bit more responsibility.'

When you are leading that small group, don't you become a monopolist, a one-man show. Jesus was a master at involving people. *'Who do men say that I am? Who do you say that I am?'*, He asks.

I have often been to services when the supposed leader chose the songs, prayed the prayers, took an offering, preached and the rest of us sat and dutifully watched while he performed. Don't be like that. Produce new leaders from your small group. Trust, give responsibility, rely on those people. It's thrilling and satisfying when you have put your life in, and then you see what, under God, you have played some part in producing. Every now and again someone will turn round and bite off your hand. You'll be tempted to say, 'All I did for them. I gave myself. I loved them. Just think of my input in their lives. Look at it! What a thankless task! I want to quit.' Don't! Keep leading; you chose them. God gave them to you and He's the rewarder – don't forget that. Don't forget either that one of the twelve was called Judas Iscariot.

Chapter 7

Leadership and My Own Actions
Myself

One of the most difficult things for a leader to resist is the wrong expectation of others. A most helpful remark made by Gerald Coates one day has since been oft-quoted by me. It was, 'Don't fall into the trap of living your life constantly as others think you should. You won't succeed.'

There are right expectations of others but often people think they know much better where you should be, and what you should be doing than ever you will. They will even know better than God. If you allow them to dictate totally to you, you won't live, let alone lead.

When I first moved to the London area I took the trouble of enquiring from the elders and deacons what they expected of a pastor. The response was quite amazing, for everyone had an opinion, and when you put all the opinions together, just to perform that which was required would have needed ten men, not one leader. What was even stranger was that most of the things they thought I should be doing personally, I didn't think I should be doing at all!

Many people know what I should be doing, or have planned, but they don't know what I am doing. Some think they know where I am and I'm probably somewhere else. Often people expect me to support, attend, pay for, be there for what they are doing when I'm quite happy to leave it with them and have no intentions of being there.

There are in Christian circles what I call the moral blackmailers, or the spiritual blackmailers. Their aim is to do two things:

1. Get rid of their own bad conscience on you by making you feel unspiritual.
2. Get you to do what they think you should be doing, usually what they don't want to do, and certainly don't want to do by themselves. However, they will feel better if they have made you do it.

I'm not sure about others but I find it hard when people say we must pray more, fast more, read the Bible more, come to this night of prayer or that day of study. Often it's not that I believe prayer, Bible study, Bible reading is wrong, I'm just not available for that one. It also puzzles me to know why it's more spiritual to pray from 10 pm to 6 am than from 6 pm to 2 am! I guess that praying through the night seems more exciting and I am not against that providing it is not seen as super-spiritual the later it is. I'm also puzzled why it's spiritual to pray all night and miss work to sleep the next day!

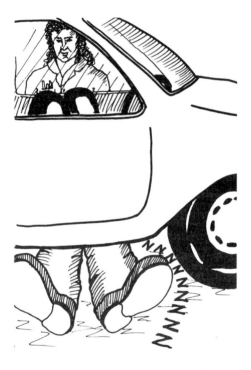

'Another prayer meeting last night, Jo?'

When I was at Bible College there was a serious young zealot who loved to pray. Due to my unspirituality, I guess, I shared a room with him. He would pray all night very hard and very loud keeping the rest of us unspiritual ones awake and restless. Then the next day we would be covering for his work period, taking notes for him in the lectures he couldn't attend and generally protecting him while he peacefully slept the night's warfare away. I'm not criticizing; I just have to confess I don't understand. I do feel though that I need to resist such pressure to make me conform to the same standards.

What you are is what you will produce. If you don't talk with God you won't lead others to do so. If you don't know your Bible those you lead won't either. If you are not consistent, reliable, trustworthy then those you lead won't be either. However, be careful that you do not allow other people's definition of spirituality to push you along a road that you have not reasoned out for yourself. Leaders must lead, not simply follow the trend or act on an emotional response to a situation.

There is the danger in the Christian Church to always wish to formalise. This is how it is done. This is the way we do it. It is very hard, however, to formalise love. The manuals can tell the men that wives need to be told they are loved. If in a morning I come downstairs with the book's instruction in my mind that I must tell my wife I love her, and I formally do so every morning, by saying 'Good morning wife, I love you,' it would become meaningless and irritating.

We need to pray/talk to God because the Bible says so, but we need to do so because we want to do so. If we do, others will follow the lead naturally.

Be aware of what you are as a person. A river never rises above its source but in terms of the group you lead you are the springhead. Be what you want those you are leading to be!

Chapter 8

Leadership and Your Testimony
My story

One of the most powerful things that you have is your own story; what happened to you. Don't be afraid of sharing it. If you notice, on Paul's best preaching engagements he usually opted to give his testimony. It was the most powerful thing that had happened to him and people find it very difficult to argue with and refute personal experience.

One of the main dangers is to dress up our story. You know the sort of thing I mean: 'I was on drugs, into the fast life, scraping the dregs of the world and then at seven years old I became a Christian!'

If you come from a good Christian home with sound, well-balanced parents who love you and brought you up well, use that part of your story with powerful effect. If on the other hand you really did get trapped into wasting a great deal of your life before you came to your senses and responded to the tug of the love of God, well then use that to good effect too.

Isn't it surprising that in many situations the most important asset is underplayed? Our story is tremendously interesting, yet it is often given bad position, and even when used it is used badly. So herewith my very own contribution of how to give a testimony, or the do's and don'ts of testifying.

Don't exaggerate. For those who don't know it already, exaggerations are lies.

Do tell the truth because you've got used to what happened to you. It doesn't maybe sound so dynamic but actually it's powerful and the Holy Spirit will use your story to effect change on people's lives. Remember always that people are reading your life as well as listening to your story.

Don't always say the same thing like a parrot.

Do remember that your story is a continuing one and God is still working with you. He hasn't finished His production so keep people up to date with what's happening.

Don't say 'Oh not me, you don't want to hear from me. You've heard it before. I'm sorry it's me.'

Do rejoice in every God-given opportunity to encourage people in the Kingdom.

Don't go on and on and on and on.

Do stand up, speak up clearly, and shut up.

'I was on drugs, into fast living and then at seven I became a Christian.'

Chapter 9

Leadership and a Platform
The public view

It will be true to say you are on a platform even if you don't want to be. It's no good saying, 'I'm only human.' You have been given by God a responsibility to lead and that's a privilege. You had better respond well to that, for to whoever much is given, much is also required.

While God will certainly deal with us as individuals, He will also require of leaders or under-shepherds to answer for what we have done in terms of leading people correctly, and He will require us to answer for what they have received at our hands.

However, this chapter is not intended to be about that sort of platform, the sort that other people put you on in their minds or opinions, but the ones you stand on to lead services, preach or whatever else you might do on them.

I have some important things to say that I haven't read anywhere else.

Leading or Chairing a Meeting

I have pet hates here. I loathe to hear people talk about preliminaries in Christian get-togethers. People say things like, 'Well, we'll get there when the preliminaries are over' or 'I hope they cut the preliminaries short' or let's get over the preliminaries and on to whatever is considered important.' I suppose that by 'preliminaries' people mean boring things, useless things or unnecessary things.

I reckon if they are boring, useless or unnecessary then we shouldn't have them at all. I believe when I'm leading a service there are no such things as preliminaries, everything is important, from the natter with the people the moment I meet them, through praise and worship, and in any giving that takes place.

In fact, even the important statements of what the army of God is doing locally, usually called announcements, are all worthwhile, important, needed and not mere preliminaries. If you have had preliminaries in the past, don't anymore. Only do what is important!

Pet hate number two is people who stand on platforms and apologise for being there saying such things as, 'I'm sorry you have to listen to me.' If they're sorry, why should I listen? Or 'I really can't speak and I don't know why I'm here.' Don't plague me then; if you can't speak, don't!

Most of these sort of attitudes are false humility. Much better to acknowledge the fact. Here is a God-given opportunity to be here. God help me to use it effectively and wisely. God, inspire me by the Holy Spirit to be Your instrument on this occasion. Don't apologise, get on with it and thank God for the opportunity.

Pet hate number three is people who over-organise or lead a meeting in such a way that it leaves no time to praise, preach, pray or whatever because they are so busy talk, talk, talking. Both leaders of meetings and often-times preachers need that useful prayer, 'God, fill my mouth with useful stuff, and nudge me when I've said enough.'

On a platform you can hinder or help. Make space for the Holy Spirit to move on people's lives. Some do's and don'ts I find helpful:

1. **Don't** look at the ceiling or the floor; **do** look at people and make eye contact.
2. **Don't** insult people with such things as 'that was awful' or 'what an ugly lot you are'; **do** lift them up, encourage, make positive statements, such as 'that was great; let's do it even better.'

3. **Don't** make silly jokes at the expense of people. That doesn't mean we shouldn't be humorous. God certainly made us with a sense of fun, so **do** be humorous.

4. **Don't** go on and on and on; **do** know when it's time to stop. **Don't** on the other hand cut the meeting short too soon; **do** be sensitive to the leading of the Holy Spirit.

5. **Do** not be afraid to go further if God is dealing with people; **don't** be afraid to finish early if it's all done.

6. **Don't** let others take charge of the meeting from you, if God has placed you in charge; **do** take charge firmly.

7. **Don't** just do things because they have to be done, such as 'it's Wednesday night and we always do it this way on Wednesday' – well, perhaps it's time to stop doing it like that; **do** rather seek to be sensitive, always listening and hearing the direction of the Holy Spirit. He may well want to cut across all your norms and traditions as He often wants to do.

Chapter 10

Leadership and Preaching
What do I say?

I do believe it is possible to learn to speak clearly, concisely, with good diction in a way that can be clearly understood and is interesting.

People are strange, aren't they? When I was in Bible College those who in my opinion were the most difficult to follow speech-wise always resisted instruction.

I don't believe there is anything we do at which we can't get better. In some circles preaching has been something that happens. It is from God, so don't try to do it better. Those of us who do preach, stand on platforms, narrate, know when we have been off and know that, notwithstanding the anointing of the Holy Spirit, we can improve. The Bible tells us it is possible to improve the use of spiritual gifts, and as that is so, then I'm sure we can improve our platform presentation.

There are lots of serious tomes on preaching. My small chapter is not an in-depth study on the subject, as I'm sure you will have already noted, but as a preacher I can say what I think. I've got some pet hates and here they are:

I hate the attitude that says – and I heard it many times as a teenager – 'I don't believe in preparation. I just let the Holy Spirit use me.' Well, if the Holy Spirit did use them, all I can say is He (the Holy Spirit) must be very dry and worn, and I don't really believe the Holy Spirit is like that.

I also hate the attitude that prepares what I call 'glass case sermons', which require people to say 'how nice' but they don't do much to you, make you do anything, go on anywhere or change your lifestyle.

I hate the attitude that prepares sermons about the furniture and the temple when people are fighting in their families because they don't know how to live.

I hate sermons that cause the preacher to say 'finally' for the fiftieth time.

It should be obvious to those of us who have aspirations to lead that we do some funny things when we are called on to speak publicly, like saying 'right, OK' after each sentence, or taking our glasses off and on so much so that it drives people to distraction, buttoning or unbuttoning our coat in nervous frustration all the time.

Sometimes we need a good friend to tell us about our eccentricities so that we can take control. Having two daughters and a son who consider their commission in life is to keep me humble and down-to-earth, I often see my own idiosyncrasies being copied at home. I know exactly how many times I hoist my trousers!

What is preaching anyway? George Canty said,

> 'Preaching is not teaching, orating, explana-tion of Scripture or feeding the sheep. It may involve all of those things, but preaching is a supernatural release of the Holy Spirit.'

I am preaching into the real lives of people to effect change and I'll continue to go with that.

To express some practical and positive views about preaching, I do believe that preaching should be done to effect change in people's lives, some immediately requiring an appeal. I know in some areas appeals are not in vogue but I reckon when people make physical movement in response to emotion the will is going to do something.

Some things do not require an appeal but do require acting on to grow, go on, mature, be different in some area or another. Some would feel I've missed it, I'm sure, but I find it hard to understand any preaching that doesn't expect some sort of change. It seems useless to me otherwise.

Spurgeon said to his trainee preachers, 'Always have two things in mind when preparing to preach – death and eternity.' I think that could wonderfully focus our attention.

For those who are beginning, I offer them advice, trusting it to be helpful. Don't try and put the whole counsel of God into a half-hour sermon. Do try and know at least what your first sentence is and if at all possible make it count.

When I was working for radio for a short time we were taught the following:

> You can make people mad, sad, happy, angry or even violently disagree and they won't switch you off. If you bore them, they will.

So in radio the first couple of seconds of the programme you have to think to yourself, there might be a hand stretching out to turn the switch and I'll not be heard. Preaching is not much different. People have a minute switch by the left ear which when pressed enables them to look at you with rapt attention and not hear a word. The switch can be automatically activated in some church fellowships by the word 'announce-ment'. Try not to switch people off in your first sentence.

Do keep to basic simple things that show you know what you're talking about. It's awful to hear young preachers going on and on about something they haven't got a clue about.

Do be sensitive to the Holy Spirit. I, of course, think you should prepare but if God wants to do something else when you get up, our attitude should be, 'That's alright with me, Lord.' Sensitivity means listening to Him, so we need our ears tuned into His voice, and then we need courage to respond.

I'll never forget being invited to lecture at a church. The Holy Spirit spoke to me and said, after my long preparation I hasten to add, 'Don't lecture on that, preach on this.' I obeyed. Being a total stranger to the fellowship I assumed that the Holy Spirit knew what was needed better than I did. At the end of our time together there were many in the congregation openly weeping. It was obvious that God knew what He was doing, even if I did not. Being a stranger I handed over to the leader of the church having finished the preach which I substituted for the lecture I was supposed to give. He obviously wasn't being sensitive to the Holy Spirit. He stood up and said, 'Any questions?' I suppose that's what you would do after a lecture, wouldn't you?

Do also know as a general rule what is your last sentence, the finale, where you end, how to stop so that you don't preach people into blessing and out again. So that you don't go on and on and on and on...

Chapter 11

Leadership and the Family
At home

What happens at home is going to affect everything else you do. The question that some people ask, 'Did you get out of bed the wrong side?' has more reality in it than we would sometimes care to admit.

No wonder the Bible teaches us that if we are to lead we first of all need to lead at home.

Home is where it happens. If we can't get it together there, there will be knock-on problems in all that we do.

I find some amazing things in this area, like a leader (supposed to be anyway) who came to me to tell me he couldn't get his eleven year old to go to school. 'He won't do what I ask,' he told me. I was fascinated and had a great many problems trying to comprehend how he was expected to lead others when his own eleven year old child could not be led.

I find it strange. I'm sure they find it a stress, when couples say to me, 'Well my husband leads, but I don't have anything to do with what he does.'

What goes on between husband and wife, wife and children, children and father will all have an effect on our leadership. It will put us in unresponsive moods if it is bad. It will encourage us if it is good.

I guess it needs a lot more space, almost separate treatment to discuss the family, a whole new book no less. There is good stuff on the market, I'm sure. Suffice to say here, I believe that in leadership, home should be a joint effort. Wife alongside husband, children alongside too. Nothing short of that joint effort will really give you the edge in leadership terms. To have that alongsideness there will need to be some very important things in the home.

There will need to be friendship; friendship between husband and wife, friendship with the children.

I reckon we treat children too much like children. We need a better word like small adult. So many families seem to see the small adults as **something** rather than **someone**; something to do things for and to, rather than a person who is part of the family and makes a total contribution to something special – the unit called the family, the place called home.

Not that children should rule as I see in some homes even before they can talk. The king sits in a high chair and directs the family by screams and gestures. A child is a person who has a contribution to make to this God-given element of family life.

'OK, How much will it cost me this time to get you to school?'

There will need to be communication and understanding. That is totally inseparable with good friendship.

There will need to be respect that is mutual both between husband and wife and the children.

There will need to be love.

In the Godhead there has always been love. That love has flared out and I'm one of the recipients of His love.

Family love will enable leadership to take place, cause other lives to be blessed and enable others to trust and to follow.

We need a flare-out of family love to the world in which we live. It's in short supply.

Chapter 12

Leadership and Vision

Goals

'Where there is no vision the people perish.'
(Proverbs 29:18)

I equate vision with goals, not simply seeing
some apparition, though I don't rule those sort
of visions out of course. Vision is the ability to
see what is and yet envisage what it is going
to become. If you have no vision or goal and you
are already in leadership your leadership will
cause the people, and the situation, to perish.
You are in charge of mediocrity. You are the
beginnings of death.

A Canadian friend of mine, Danny Moe,
used to lecture on being positive at all sorts of
big management meetings and sales meetings, as
well as Christian gatherings. He told me that less
than 1% have any real goal. Most are just doing

a job. If you want to lead you need to get into that 1%.

Some years ago I had the privilege of visiting a large newspaper and being shown around the plant. I looked at production, dispatch, accounts, the computer and finally had lunch with the chief editor.

In the middle of lunch I remember asking my favourite question, 'What are your goals for this newspaper?' He almost choked on his meal. 'Goals?' he said, 'what do you mean? Can't you see what we have done?' 'Oh yes,' I said 'but I'm also interested in what you're going to do.' If the past is impressive then the future should also be exciting. Sadly he didn't have any goals. He was just keeping shop.

Leadership must not only be aware of where it has come from; it should be conscious of where it is. It must also know where it is going.

Don't tell me you are just waiting on God, and the Lord knows that wherever He wants you to go that's fine by you, because friend, that is another cop-out for mediocrity.

Jesus said He wants us as friends, and He wants us as friends so we can understand where we are going together. So you'd better get some goals and vision within the broad plan of where God is going.

So often, it seems our vision has not been higher than a second storey roof.

I believe that because God is a big God and He is working with us and through us, we ought therefore to have big goals and a large vision. So often, it seems, our vision has not been higher than a second storey roof. We have tended therefore to hit the first floor ceiling. At least if we aim for the moon we should at least get to the top of the roof or even a bit higher than that.

When you begin to talk about vision or goals a strange sort of paralysis sets in on people.

The first kind of paralysis goes something like this:

> 'I want to lead 10,000 people. I only have 6 at the moment. What a foolish thought that was.' We stop there and forget it.

A large vision or a far-off goal must be broken down into bite-size achievable objectives. If I want 10,000 people and only have 6 I need to set the first target for 12. I need to take small steps that will be in line with my ultimate goal. It will not do just to have the vision in mind. I must then begin to plan the route to get to that vision. As the Chinese say, 'every long journey starts with the first step.'

The second kind of paralysis sounds like this:

> 'I want 10,000 people. I only have 6. My first step is to get 12 people.' End of thought.

It needs to go further than that; we then need to set objectives as to how we will get those 12 people. We will need also to set time limits otherwise we will be dead before we have moved anywhere. How long is it going to take me to get 12, 24, 48, 96, 192, 384 etc.? Sometimes we won't hit those deadlines but if you set them, at least you know you missed and can try again.

The tragedy is that many leaders want to

have target practice but they definitely do not want a target.

Elsewhere in this little book I have used the phrase 'Holy ambitions'. I believe we need it in our personal life and if we plan to lead we need it for those whom we are leading.

The next phase of establishing a vision or goal is what the church growth people call persuading others to share your goal, or goal owning. It is important as leaders that not only do we have a goal or vision but that we also succeed in selling that goal or vision to the people we are leading; not only the ultimate vision but the next objective to reach on the way. Those you lead will then become 'goal owners' with you. It will cease to be your goal but will become their goal, our goal.

My goal is owned by my friends, family and team. They don't see it as mine, it's theirs. They want to go where I want to go and I want to go where God wants to go.

It's time to set up the match well enough, so that when we score all of us can get in to the excitement of shouting, '**Goal!**'

Chapter 13

Leadership and Production
Work and pass on

Paul, writing to Timothy, told him to pass on what he knew to teach faithful men so they could teach others. Leaders need to be producers.

Some years ago I had problems with one or two people whom we were leading, in that they had problems with my use of the word 'project'. They somehow felt that we ought to be into worshipping God, not into projects. 'Get into people, not into projects.' I'm into worshipping God but not just when the Church meets together. I believe that our whole lives should bring Him praise and what we produce should be offered to Him as worship. Paul tells us that he is going to offer to God those he has brought into the Kingdom.

A good project is one that will bless people, help people, touch people in need, and demonstrate the love of God through those you lead in practical ways, ways that will draw people to you and ultimately enable you to offer those people to God as part of your worship.

So leaders need to have projects. I define a project this way:

> It is the next step or action in the line of steps which will enable me to reach my **ultimate** goal.

It may be a building we need. It may be some new kind of follow-up system. It may be some new initiative to take, but it will be a step towards my/our ultimate goal.

Leaders need to be innovative, to see that which others have thrown away, seemingly useless, and yet see what it can become for the Kingdom.

I remember having bought, on behalf of our fellowship, some derelict buildings in North London as part of the development of our Newriver fellowship. Having signed the contract we had a thanksgiving service. God had enabled us to acquire the property, so all the fellowship stood around praising and thanking God for His enablement. My small son, as he was then, turned round to my wife and said, 'Has my dad gone mad? Why is he thanking God for these buildings? They are all broken.' Well, I took his point, but someone must be able to see what can be produced from the mess. Certainly God saw it with reference to our lives.

Leaders are, or should be, producers.

We should always be dreaming, planning, scheming (apologies to my American friends for the word scheming) to bring in the next step. As you do that, you ought also to discover that leaders are not in the juggling business. You should not try to hold every scheme, every project, every new plan all at the same time.

As a programme gets under way you should have those you are teaching and training ready to come in and take over, ready to cement, to develop and establish that which you have begun so that you can move on to the next step, gradually taking your hand off that area and trusting the new leader to continue to develop, to have his own dreams, vision and plans for that which was once your baby. It should continue to be a sharing process, but one which you do not feel 'I have to, under God, make this happen.'

Someone else under God is now making that happen. They are developing, enlarging, establishing your vision. Let them do it.

Leaders must produce. What are you producing? It needs to happen in the lives of people in the things that the group usually does. In terms of Kingdom conquest we are in the Production Business.

Chapter 14

Leadership and Children
Spiritual children

If we are in any sort of growth situation (and if we are not then we ought to be), we need to produce other new leaders. The best way of doing that is to have sons and daughters. Not just physical ones but spiritual ones.

I am convinced, and have been for some time now, that the best form of training is 'on the job' training in the practice and the place where one is to lead; home-grown leadership in other words.

That doesn't mean they should never go away, but I am convinced that in church life in the past we have sent our young leaders away far too soon: off to Bible College or some other place for two, three or four years. What happens is that roots are lost. It becomes difficult to re-settle and pick up the threads of local leadership.

Ministries travel away from a culture and when they get back to that culture they seem alienated. They have grown apart. Even from one area of the country to another the culture, thinking, attitudes and economy change. It's not impossible of course to slot in, but harder than if you train in the environment you plan to lead in.

Training is more than lectures or theory, it needs to lean on experience. Training for spiritual leadership is more than a hands-on experience. It requires spiritual fathers and mothers.

So how do you adopt a son or daughter in this sense?

I suppose it comes down to areas of realisation of potential and an extension of friendship. Once the two areas have been established I believe the following should take place.

First, time must be spent with the son or daughter, not just lecture time or training time but friendship time.

Second, take the person in tow. Take them with you wherever you go, expose them to all that you do, share the joys, expectations, God's aims and your disappointments. Let them see what you get up to inside your home as well as out of it. In other words not only get them to know your job but to know you as well.

Third, give them real responsibility. Trust them to take areas from you; let them know that you trust them. Give them charge; trust them with leadership.

Fourth, make provision for practical and theoretical training as you would for your physical children in terms of school etc.

Fifth, if necessary (it may not be but if it is), see that they are exposed to other people with recognised leadership in the Kingdom.

Sixth, give them heavy chunks of your responsibility and take your hands off (what you hold you lose anyway). What you give up for the Kingdom comes back in some way.

Seventh, enjoy the fruit of expanding leadership.

It's probably not as easy as handing over the responsibility of training to someone else, it will cost in personal time and effort. It definitely seems to be how Jesus did it and it's most rewarding.

Chapter 15

Leadership and Other Leaders

Loyalty

Leadership with other leaders is probably the key to the whole effective understanding and operation of leadership. If we learn this I reckon we will go a long way. Its wrong application and understanding has, in my opinion, caused the work of God in certain countries to fail to reach their full heights of effectiveness.

This is probably particularly true in western countries where of recent years we have got so used to thinking democratically that we think this is a Christian thing to do. This thinking, of course, has pervaded the Church in the western world. I probably won't be popular for pointing it out, but God never seems interested in taking a vote. God doesn't even seem interested in voting when there is an important appointment of men or women to lead whole multitudes of people being made, even when they are leading nations.

So Moses gets the job, appointed by God. No vote, no election and even, dare we say, against popular opinion. 'We don't want you here,' they told Moses, 'You're getting us into trouble.' He stayed anyway!

A cry of 'crucify' may have been majority rule; it might have been mob rule; it might have been a simple majority at that time, but Jesus Christ is still Lord and King. The Father has said so and that's that. I have sat in church and listened to the key to this leadership question being totally missed. I believe the key is seen in Matthew chapter eight, which is the story of the centurion whose servant was sick. The Roman to whom Jesus said, *'What great faith.'*

This guy knew a thing or two. I have listened to not a few preachers say, 'The centurion **had** authority' and that he recognised that Jesus Christ also had authority. Perhaps you have read Matthew 8:9 correctly, but even so the understanding of it has got to be applied in daily life.

The Roman centurion actually said, *'I am a man **under authority**'* or as the Amplified Bible says *'subject to authority.'* Let's spell that out. That meant in hard everyday terms he was a man who knew he had to do what he was told; who knew he was responsible to others; who knew that he was not a law unto himself; who knew that he was not there by the popular vote. He knew he had to answer for his actions to a higher authority than his own; he knew that he was not in an independent movement of one; he knew that the higher authority had also given him authority and Jesus, of course, said of Himself,

> *'I did not come to do my own will but the will of the Father who sent me.'*

Leadership, even if you have a potential for it, will never arrive until it learns to do as it is told. So in leadership we need to know we are under authority and it's a cop out to say 'I know I'm under God'; we need to be under others too. We need also to be subject one to another. That's the key. Now if we have learned to turn the key right then we will find we have a respect for fellow leaders who we perceive are on the same level as us. We will respect their ministries, take note of what they can't do, so that we can help them and take note of what we can't do and invite them to help us.

We will also be loyal; I love that word; so many are not loyal. When you find those who are, they're a prize indeed.

When we have turned the Matthew eight key correctly we will be willing to have respect for those who God has set over us, not in a blind obedient sort of way, but a respectful, responsive, loyal way. We shall also be aware of those who lead but are perhaps not on the same ladder of leadership as we are; those who we feel that, whilst they are leading others, we nevertheless are leading them. We shall, if we have turned the key correctly, see ways to enhance their leadership, pull them up to our level or even replace ourselves with them or, dare I say, perhaps push them beyond and above us.

Chapter 16

Leadership and Friends
Solomon's clothes

When I was in Bible College (I hope it's changed), as a group of students working towards leadership of churches we were constantly instructed not to get too close to those who were members of the Fellowship. I remember that we were told that leadership is a lonely life. You musn't get too friendly with people, you need to keep aloof. Some of those ideas will have changed I hope, and pray, but as late as 1985/86 I've heard reports from my wife and fellow ministers who tell me that many in full-time leadership assume that loneliness and lack of friends is still equal to some sort of advanced spirituality. I don't believe it is.

Right from the day I started out as a pastor in the North of England (Grangetown,

Middlesbrough) I couldn't for the life of me see how I was to minister to a group of people effectively without being friends. I needed to be friends with them and some of them I really liked, still like and still count as my friends. I broke all the rules, I got involved. Some of them liked me. I obviously didn't make my spiritual quota because I didn't feel lonely and neither did my wife.

I remember Pauline going to a ministers' wives fraternity around that time, returning and incredulously telling me, 'They all cried, they've got no friends. I feel so sorry for them because we've got lots.'

The Bible says *'he who would have friends let him also be friendly.'* I don't find any Scripture to base doctrine on the theory that leaders shouldn't have friends.

The cry that will still be heard in reply to this is that for a leader to have friends will cause favouritism, jealousy etc. Well, they are bad things to have, but that doesn't make having friends wrong. It does make that sort of jealousy wrong and that perception of favouritism.

It seems that God has always been in the business of close friends in order to bless the masses. *'Abraham, my friend,'* He says. John constantly refers to himself in his gospel as *'the disciple whom Jesus loved.'* Exclusive friendship?

Well, yes, in a way, so that there could also be inclusive blessing to the nations.

I want to be a friend of His. I guess how special depends on how much time I give to Him. It will depend on how much I want to do the things He wants to do; how much I get in tune, but that's always how it is with friends.

The subject of this chapter is Solomon's clothes. I've talked about this subject to many people. Often they look at you very curiously, especially when I say to people, 'You want to improve your marriage? You need to understand Solomon's clothes. You want to get on in business? You need to understand Solomon's clothes. You want your leadership to be enhanced? You need to understand Solomon's clothes.' When you say those things people think you're just a little off beam. How can Solomon's clothes have anything to do with marriage?

A young lady came to me one day in the church at Newriver and said, 'Adrian, you know I'm courting and you know the man; you know I think I have a problem. He wants me to stop ministering in my own way.' This young lady had quite a ministry too. She said, 'What shall I do?' Well it was a long conversation but basically I said, 'Unless you can get him to understand Solomon's clothes, I should give him up. It won't work.' She couldn't persuade him to see it, and she did give him up. She's happily married to someone else now and going on with God.

So what's so important about these clothes? Patience, patience. You will find the reference to the said Solomon's clothes in 1 Kings chapter 10, which outlines the visit of the Queen of Sheba to Solomon's court. I understand from the experts that in those days it was good practice in following the crowd that the trend in all kings' palaces was that kings sat on thrones dressed in the finest apparel that money could buy. Nothing unusual about that. Servants on the other hand were dressed as dully as possible and always stood up. I suppose the drabness of the one was supposed to rivet your attention on the finery of the king. It probably seemed like putting a candle in Wembley Stadium on a very dark night.

Solomon was a wise character. Note 1 Kings chapter 10 verse 4. The Queen of Sheba heard about Solomon's great skill and wisdom, then in verse 5, his food, and here it is, the description of his officers, and the apparel of his servants. The Queen, we are told, was breathless and overcome. Solomon sat many of his officials down and dressed his servants in the best that there was. Wise man! That was like floodlights in Wembley Stadium. He lifted up those around him and he was not pushed down by that act but lifted up even higher. The enhancement of others usually leads to our own increase.

There's a strange quirk of our usual human activity that makes us choose friends who subconsciously we feel won't outshine us in dress, ideas or behaviour, a sort of 'servant in grey clothes, a leader-in-red syndrome'.

When we have learned the principles of Solomon's clothes we will make friends of those who we are sure are going ahead, strong, well able and dressed in gold; we shall make friends of those who, perhaps at this point in time, we are stronger than, but we shall seek in every way to enhance, encourage, and improve their position. Our world often stands on those who are perceived as lower, that they might get higher. Actually all that happens is that we all sink lower. In God's economy we need to push those above us up higher still, rejoice with them in their success, and then pull up those who are perceived as lower. We will then discover that we are all moving up.

I'm always suspicious of leaders who have to look smart and trendy but make their wives look 'spiritual' and drab, or wives that sparkle while they persuade their men to be boring. Remember Solomon's clothes. Let's be lifter-uppers.

Chapter 17

Leadership and Style
The changing you

If your goal is set, if your vision is ahead and if you have taken the first step, maybe more than the first steps, then you can look back and see where you have come from.

You must then know that there is not only change taking place in those you lead, and in the situation those you lead find themselves, but there must be a change in you too. In some ways it seems unnecessary to say this. The strange thing about human beings is that we want things to change, but we don't want them to be different. Things must change, and when they do they will be different.

This chapter nearly didn't get written and I thought, 'surely people must know this fact?' I then thought, 'how do you know it?' I know it because I experience it and because others have said it, but also I tried to resist it and could not!

Your leadership style must change along with the development of those you lead and with the changing situation.

It is different to lead 6 than 12, 30 than 300, 300 than 1,000. The style must change.

In a large company there are charge hands, foremen, supervisors, department managers, area managers, middle managers, directors, managing directors. It should be obvious that the charge hand is a leader of people and that the managing director is a leader of people. Work is achieved through people. If the managing director of a company employing thousands of people has the style of management or leadership that is the same as the charge hand then the company is going to be in trouble.

If you are leading 12 people and you plan to meet on Saturday at 6.00 pm you can phone all 12, you could visit all 12 and say, 'Be there.' It takes much longer to visit 30 or even to 'phone them. You might therefore duplicate a letter. You will know the names of 30 to 100 people reasonably well, but try and remember the names of 300 or 1,000.

You might profitably use your leadership in duplicating letters for 50 people but try doing it for 500.

You might take pride in writing a personal note to all of the 100 people that you are responsible for leadership of, but try doing it to 1,000.

So many times leaders fail to see that a changing situation has taken place, and because they fail to see it they fail to move on themselves.

Leaders tend to try to handle their own lives when leading 600 as they did when they had 60. This will lead to confusion, misinformation and

It takes much longer to visit 30, or even to 'phone them.

bad organisation. Actually you won't ever get to 600 if your leadership style does not change.

Each time you aim to grow to lead more, know also that your style must change. Plan now how you will change that style, in ways that will leave your hands free for future advancement, and in ways that will enable you to bring the best to the people whom you lead. For those of you who do read books, and I guess you do if you're reading this one, may I recommend a book called, *The Pyramid Principle of Church Growth*. It deals with the different styles of leadership.

There are three choices in leadership style: stay as you are and allow the group you lead to be the same size, and to a certain extent sterile; hand over leadership to someone whose style will enlarge the group, or take it further than you can, or are willing to. Better still, learn to change your style.

I personally pray you will opt for change.

Chapter 18

Leadership and Power
God in us

Where does leadership come from? Right at the beginning of this little book I tried to give some sort of definition of leadership. Some leaders are appointed, some should not be. In my heart I do believe that to lead in the Kingdom we need to be called of God.

The problem with that statement is that most of us have a subjective view of what constitutes a call from God. Some will expect an audible voice from Heaven saying, 'Go and lead in ... land.' Others will look for an angel on a fluffy white cloud which will float down in front of them and then proclaim, 'Go to Bible College.'

I suppose it might be one of those two ways, but if we limit it to that then I'm sure we will miss it.

There are lots of things that constitute a

call: the need, the desire, the ambition, the strategy, the potential and the ability. The trouble is that having all or some of those things is not necessarily the call of God for a specific task.

The Bible tells us to seek first the Kingdom. If we seek to know God, and the most important thing in all the world to us is knowing Him, and if we really have a love affair with the King, then we shall begin to clarify and understand what He wants.

In human relationships, good ones that is, a married couple ought to be able to get to the position where what the wife wants is what the husband wants to give, and what the husband wants to do is what the wife would like to do.

In terms of the call of God, if we know God, if we love God, if He loves us – and He most certainly does – then what we are called to do becomes a strange question. We shall know what God's plans are. We will understand His purposes. We will understand what we are in Him, what can be accomplished in Him, and we will get on and do it.

Some will perhaps think me irreverent here, but I do believe it works like this.

God has a plan, but it is not so narrow a plan that we need to look through a piece of macaroni to view it. It's a broad plan and when we come to God with areas of the plan which interest us or particularly inspire us and say, 'Father, what would you like me to do concerning this?' to the surprise of many God the Father is likely to reply, 'What would you like to do?'

We then might say, 'Father, what is your purpose here?' and the Father will say, 'What do you think?' I don't believe God has made us into robots or machines. He is interested in what we think.

I'm a lot older than my children. I have a greater experience of life, I hope! I probably know much more where I am and where I'm going than they do, but I still want to know what they think. I'm still interested in their opinions, and I'm still very happy when they make independent decisions, even if sometimes they are not the specific decisions I would have made for them.

The Father, of course, will hold our hands, pick us up when we fall and comfort and encourage, but He does also want us to walk ourselves.

There are times, of course, when we need to hear the Father say, 'Well, I know that's what you would plan to do, it's the way you would go, but your sight is limited. From my bird's-eye view I can see that the decision, plan, action is going to give you greater problems than you need down the road.'

'Walk round the walls of Jericho,' He says to Joshua. *'Take only 300 men,'* He says to Gideon and see the salvation of the Lord. God wants us to be planners, visionaries, God-inspired activists, but He also wants us to listen, and when He says, 'Just a minute, do it this way this time,' I'm with Him!

Chapter 19

Leadership and Rewards
Benefits

I hope by now we are coming out of the attitude that a leader needs to be kept poor and humble and, by inference, spiritual.

If we are to lead effectively we must understand that God our Father is going to look after us. He has promised if we seek first the Kingdom then the other things will be added unto us. What are the other things? I believe they are the practical things to do the job: money, equipment, clothing, and a place to live. These things are often not luxuries, they are needs.

It seems sad to me that in the past Christian leaders have assumed that we have to use the leftovers. I recognise that we must start somewhere and the best place to start is with what you have got. Don't wait until you have got the best equipment before you do anything. On the other hand don't settle for using that cheap equipment for ever. Plan to upgrade, improve. This is Kingdom business and it deserves the best there is. If you don't use what you've got you won't get anything better.

So why do we do what we do? Why do we lead? Not for money, but don't be afraid to receive that. You need it to live and if you're always worrying about the next month you won't be concentrating on the Kingdom; not for the up-to-date equipment, though we need that; not for the best places to live, but I want to be comfortable at home; not for human congratulations, though some of that will come and when it does, please don't turn round and say, 'Don't thank me, give God the Glory.' We need encouragement. Receive it when it is given and say thank you nicely. Don't be churlish and super-spiritual or spooky. Primarily it is not to please people. Sometimes we will and that's quite a good feeling which people immediately receive. You may have to lead in very difficult parts, hard battles, real tough warfare. It may not be men-pleasing at all.

So why? What is the reward? I reckon it's as we look and see changed lives, new people in Christ, the extension of the Kingdom, leaders we help to produce, but most of all it is for His, 'Well done!' That's more than enough reward.

Chapter 20

Leadership and Leading
Abandoning mediocrity

So if you have embarked on a course of leadership, then you must lead. Abdication is always a messy business.

This is a plea for the abandonment of mediocrity. We need, particularly in the safe, secure, pensionable, insurable United Kingdom, to learn the need to be fresh, to take risks, to be radical, to desire change.

I can almost hear someone saying, 'We don't want to change for change's sake.' Actually, I have decided that clichés or oft-quoted sayings are nearly always wrong, except, that is, those that come from the Bible and then it seems to me they are often not understood. We do want change for change's sake. For change indicates growth and life. So let's constantly change for the better.

If you want to lead you must take responsibility, at least for what you think. I'm tired of
hearing phrases like, 'Well I don't know, I'll
have to see what the Board thinks.' 'I don't
know what HQ would say' (for those in
centrally-controlled denominations). 'I don't
want to commit myself in case it goes wrong.'

Well, you have to if you really want to lead,
especially if you want to be a person of principle
with vision and goals. It's your job to say where
you're going. If Moses had called an Elders
Meeting they would have stayed in Egypt. If
when things got tough he had gone back to them
for direction they would have gone back to
Egypt. Yet I often hear leaders say, 'my Board,
my HQ, my Parochial Council, my Committee,
won't let me. I want to, but they won't let me.'
You need to **lead**, man!

Where does God want you to go? What does
He want you to do? Maybe He wants you up
against the Red Sea with the armies of the enemy
pressing in behind and the folk you have led
saying what a terrible person you are for leading
them there. At least there you can either die or
see the salvation of the Lord. It's never boring
or mediocre.

God save us as leaders from the desire of
being simply pensionable, insurable and secure.
Help us to be those who have ambition. If you

are aspiring to lead and have no ambition you have no hope. I believe it's time all Christians understood what it means to have Holy Ambition – it's not wrong, it's right.

Faith is risky living; good leadership is risky, it requires us to try to be the first to see things through: to dare.

Leadership should never be in the business of simply maintaining the status quo. So many times I have seen people in committees with long faces saying, 'If you make that decision you will change the status quo.' Hooray, it probably needed changing anyway! I know there are absolutes but they are God-made. Most of the ones people get hot under the collar about are man-made.

We so easily get into censorship mood over things new. In the economy of God nothing is new and yet all things are new. Certainly they are fresh. We need to be fresh, experimental, willing to try a new approach; people who step out. Most entrepreneurs are so because they find something new or pick up something that others have looked at but never seen how to use. Leaders need an entrepreneur's approach.

Let's get out, let's have a go, take some risks, dump our fear, have faith in God and turn the world the right way up!